Achieving Heaven's Vision For Your Life

Wynne Goss

Achieving Heaven's Vision For Your Life

Pressing the 'Reset' button on the way we do church.

**PRESS TO RESET TO MANUFACTURER'S
ORIGINAL SETTINGS**

Press The Reset Button
Breaking The Cycle Forever

When something is not working, as we know it should, then we all know what to do to solve the problem. We must turn to the manufacturer's manual. The manufacturer is aware that the customer may experience a malfunction of the item, requiring assistance and guidance on how to fix any problem and get the item working to its full potential once again.

At the back of most manufacturers' manuals there is a section giving instructions on how to resolve the most common malfunctions, followed by a statement for when you have tried everything they suggest to fix the problem and yet the item still malfunctions. The statement reads something like *"Reset To Manufacturer's Original Settings."* Following these instructions will wipe away any settings you have altered over the months or years you have owned and used the item, and return it to the settings programmed into the item when you first purchased it. Resetting the item to its original settings usually means the item begins to work as originally designed by the manufacturer, and you, the customer, are once again happy to see it operating at its full potential. Nothing is worse than paying a high price for something that is not doing what the manufacturer promised it would do.

I feel Church is often like this for so many of us. We came to Christ, 'joining up' to co-work with Him in His Mission of taking the message of God's love, forgiveness, reconciliation and salvation to everyone in every part of this world. We all heard the messages, read the Bible, were stirred by the testimonies of others and expected that we would see the power of the Spirit happening all around us, as it was with Jesus, the apostles Peter and Paul, with Smith Wigglesworth, Kathryn Kuhlman and so many other great men and women of God. Sadly, this has not been the experience for so many.

Two thousand years of Church history reveal that there have been moments since those early days, that a revival and outpouring of God's power has occurred somewhere in the earth. They were so powerful that hundreds of books were written about the occasions, or about the main leaders of those moves of God. Each book was written to inspire or challenge us to rise up to believe for yet another occasion where God's Word and Spirit would move across the region, or world, with such great effectiveness, signs and wonders, bringing multitudes into the glorious freedom and liberty from sin that is available through Jesus Christ.

Going In Circles

History records the Church goes in circles, with each fresh revival of God breaking us free from religious mindsets and theology that has entrapped the Church, for sometimes hundreds of years. Each move of God brought a fresh wind of the Spirit, the people became 'on fire,' once again passionate about the Lord, His Word, His presence and sharing their faith with those who never knew Him.

Breaking The Cycle Forever

The people of each new move throw off the 'clothing' or 'style' of the 'traditional' Church, that they have left, and start new churches, new ministries, with new styles believing they are being radical in doing so. But just a generation or so later, it seems they begin to be just like the 'old' Church they came out of. They have gone in a circle. So often, they have returned to doing Church no differently than done for centuries, just with new dress codes, slightly different styles of buildings, using different musical instruments. The question we need to ask is why? Why do we have this same pattern occurring throughout our history? Well, I hope within this small book and it's message, to share with you how to break this cycle forever and allow us to see His Church fulfil its true potential.

Reformation For Realignment

It seems that the common denominator of each move of God, is that it realigns the Church back to the truth of God's Word. Each move of God restores something that had been 'lost' to the Church over the centuries.

One such occasion was the reformation of Martin Luther (1517). The global Church had drifted far from the truth of Jesus' teaching and was operating and preaching as if we were all still under the Old Covenant Law. The Church had become brutal to sinners, viciously punishing those who erred, when the very basis of the gospel of Jesus is love, mercy, forgiveness and kindness and a salvation purely through faith in Jesus Christ, not by the rules, regulations and rituals of the Old Testament Law or Church system. Our brothers and sisters were torched to death, beheaded and brutally maimed, by those calling themselves the Church of Jesus. The Church of the day was TOTALLY out of alignment with Jesus' teachings and New Testament truth. So the Lord raised up a series of leaders to realign His Church back to the New Testament model laid down by Christ and His apostles.

One such occasion was when a young priest called Martin Luther, preached that we are 'saved by grace and not our own works,' which was a total contradiction to the normal dogma of the Church in his time. He was called a heretic and persecuted by the very church he was part of. He was thrown out of the Catholic Church and therefore began holding meetings, which developed into a collection of new Churches, led by priests who had been convinced by this new teaching he was bringing to everyone.

Thousands of ordinary people flocked to these new churches with the 'new' message of grace. The reformation spread rapidly across Europe, fuelled by others also breaking ranks with the normal Church of the day. One such person was William Tyndale, who violated the rule of the Catholic Church, by translating the New Testament into English, in order for it to be read by the 'common man.' The Pope, and the Catholic Church held the strong view that the Word of God was only to be read and studied by priests who they had trained.

This new 're-formed' Church, had received revelation that demanded a response to change the Church. It did. It changed its theology. But sadly, it did not change the deeper revelation of the purpose of the Church and her mission. It was not long before this new reformed Church of Martin Luther, had it's own buildings, with services just like the Church they broke away from. They still operated with the separation of priests and laity, the priests still wearing clothing that identified them as different to the congregations. They still sang hymns, took offerings on a plate and still only one person leading and preaching the Word. This new reformation which initially offered so much hope of seeing "His Kingdom come," ended up becoming a denominational organisation. In fact, not much had changed in the way Church operated.

Today, as I write this book, it is 500 years since that reformation. Where is it now? That fire and passion to continue the work of reforming Church, has all but gone out within her.

Sadly, we see this same truth and occurrence with all former reformations. Simply look at the breakaways of the Brethren, Baptist, Methodist, Pentecostal movements and see the churches, denominations and 'streams,' once radical in their ways, now seemingly not much different from the Church they broke away from. Why?

Changing the message to be more in alignment with the truth of the New Testament is wonderful and so necessary. Changing the way we present the gospel, or do Church services to be more relevant to the culture we are trying to influence, is also wonderful.

> *But if we do not change the mindset of why the Church exists and it's true purpose, then this new 'radical' church, with it's radical presentation, will simply grow old, becoming, in essence, virtually no different to the Church expression they came out of.*

Reformation Is Not For The Faint-Hearted

We have all the beautiful buildings, wonderfully organised meetings and Church systems, the latest technology, lavish advertising, music teams, conferences, guest speakers, gifts of free turkeys for Thanksgiving or Christmas and yet, we still do not reach or effect the world around us to the measure we read in the Bible, and what we know in our spirit is possible.

So why do we keep doing Church the same way it has been done for a thousand years or more, expecting a different result? **The model is malfunctioning.** It will not reach the whole world, which is the co-mission of Jesus. It is time the Church was brave enough to press the '*Reset To Manufacturer's Original Settings*' button. Yes, it will mean a wiping away of a lot of things that have become our mindset, tradition and culture. But who do you wish to please? The God of the Church, or the Church of God?

Reformation is not for the faint-hearted, but for those whose hearts burn within, to see the return of Heaven on Earth, in every nation in this and every generation.

It really is time we accepted that doing Church in the way it is normally done, will never achieve the mandate of Jesus, which is to 'disciple the nations.' (Matt 28:19). It is time to press the 'reset' button.

Table of Contents

Chapter 1

Envision
Knowing The Heavenly Vision

Envision
Knowing The Heavenly Vision

There is a difference between Vision and Mission.
Vision is eternal and never changes. The Mission is the temporal way we bring the Vision to pass in every culture and generation. If we get confused as to what the actual Vision of God is, then our Mission will also be out of alignment. The way you begin anything determines it's outcome. What you sow is what you'll reap. We must re-learn to plant the correct 'seed,' in our understanding and communication, of what the Church really is and what Fathers purpose is for it, in order to gain the correct fruit or harvest. The fruit of the tree is the result of the seed planted in the beginning. The root determines the fruit, not vice versa;

> *"every good tree bears good fruit, but a bad tree bears bad fruit.*
> *A good tree cannot bear bad fruit, nor can a bad tree bear good*
> *fruit……..by their fruits you will know them." (Matt 7:17-20)*

So often, we the Church, establish 'Vision' in practical terms, such as size and location of a building, the numbers attending meetings, the style of worship performance, or the types of ministries that will operate in the Church. Jesus did not concern Himself with any of these things. His goals were eternal goals, not temporal ones. We see this from His first and last earthly words;

> *"From that time Jesus began to preach and say, 'Repent, for the* ***kingdom of heaven*** *is at hand.' " (Matt 4:17)*

> *"being seen by them during forty days and speaking of the things pertaining to the* ***kingdom of God*** *………Lord will You at this time restore the* ***kingdom*** *to Israel? (Acts 1:3,6)*

His first and last words were about the Kingdom of God. He focused on an eternal Kingdom, and it's extension into the hearts of people everywhere, in order to establish the values and atmosphere of His Kingdom on earth as it is in Heaven. He thought these eternal matters more important than membership, meetings, ministry or money. The disciples, on the other hand, were concerned with whether the Lord would restore the earthly and natural kingdom of Israel by delivering it from the rule of Rome. He was discussing the eternal Vision of God, but they were more consumed by concern for an earthly vision.

Love, righteousness, justice, peace, joy, faithfulness, wholeness, and such qualities, are so much greater than temporal buildings or projects. Therefore, surely it is better for each of us to focus upon seeing these qualities restored in a persons life, by reconciling them to the person of Jesus Christ, more than spending our time and efforts upon having buildings that hold meetings to talk about Him more and more. To restore a building and see it filled with those who have already been reconciled to God the Father, by His Son Jesus Christ, is wonderful. But to restore His hope, grace, righteousness and peace to a nation, and see it filled with people who are reconciled to Him, must be a greater thing for us to focus upon. Let us focus on the greater eternal thing Father is desiring restored, more than on the temporal buildings we seem so often preoccupied with.

Seek First The Kingdom of God

Are you ready to be shocked? Jesus never told anyone to build Him a Church! Yet, for centuries it seems our efforts have been consumed with starting another church somewhere. We have convinced ourselves that the answer to everyone's problems lies in us filling the nation with more churches. Sadly the answer is entirely the opposite;

"And on this rock I will build My Church." (Matt 16:18)

Jesus said He would build His Church, not us. This one simple misunderstanding, has had Church leadership of the global Church, out of alignment from Heaven's purpose for centuries. It comes as a huge shock and 'wake-up' call, to most leaders on hearing this truth, because it is all we have ever known to do and if we don't build Him a Church, then what do we do?

When Jesus declares *'I will build My Church,'* He uses the singular sense of the word, not the plural. He is building One Church, not a multitude of Churches. If we truly wish to walk with God and co-work with Him, then we need to start doing the very opposite of what we have been doing for centuries. We need to tear down every divisive wall of offence and theological reasoning that is keeping the church divided, and discover He has only ever had one Church. We are not called to work to establish unity, but work to **keep** the unity of the faith;

> *"I, therefore, the prisoner of the Lord, beseech you to walk worthy of the calling with which you were called, with all lowliness and gentleness, with long-suffering, bearing with one another in love, **endeavouring to keep the unity** of the Spirit in the bond of peace. There is one body and one Spirit, just as you were called in one hope of your calling; one Lord, one faith, one baptism; one God and Father of all, who is above all, and through all, and in you all."* (Ephesians 4:1-6).

The Church should never be divided in the first place.

Jesus, our Master-builder and Apostle, never built a physical building made with bricks or stones, with weekly attended meetings. Nor was He driven to establish more and more 'Church' activities to get more and more people busy every week doing the 'ministry' and fulfilling the vision of the pastor. Jesus built people, not Churches. I can hear you asking the question, 'Then if He builds the Church, what do we do?' Well, exactly what He told us to do 2000 years ago.

In Matthew Chapter 5 we see Jesus laid down Heavens Constitution (we have named them 'The Beatitudes'). Then in Matthew Chapter 6:9-13 Jesus teaches His disciples to pray (we have called it the Lord's Prayer). The subject matter of the opening and closing of this foundational prayer, is regarding the kingdom of God;

> *"Your **kingdom** come. Your will be done on earth as it is in Heaven.......For Yours is the **kingdom** and the power and the glory forever. Amen"* (Matthew 6:10,13).

At the end of this same Chapter of Matthew, we see Jesus releasing to us our focus and vision;

> *"Seek first the **kingdom** of God **and His righteousness**, and all these things shall be added to you." (v 33)*

When Jesus rose from the dead, He spent the next 40 days speaking to His disciples in preparation of His ascending to Heaven. You would expect Him during those vital days to tell them all how to build His Church, if this was to be their work. Yet, He mentions not one word of instruction to them regarding this issue. The narrative of the Book of Acts records Him as totally focusing the disciples on one thing only. To focus on the Kingdom of God.

> *"being seen by them during forty days and speaking of the **things pertaining to the Kingdom** of God" (Acts 1:3)*

From beginning to end, Jesus drew everyone's attention to focus on living by the Constitution of the Kingdom of God and establishing it's culture in earth, as it is in Heaven. This must always remain our focus. If we seek first the kingdom of God, then we will see Him build His Church. If we seek to build His Church, then it does not mean we will achieve the manifestation of His kingdom in our midst.

The 'Vision' for us therefore, is the revealing of the King and His Kingdom in the lives of people everywhere. Our 'Mission' is the multitude of ways we, the Church, achieve this.

The Tabernacle of Moses
The Book of Exodus and the letter to the Hebrew Christians, reveal that whilst on Mt. Sinai, Moses saw into Heaven, and beheld the real tabernacle of God. The word 'tabernacle' means '**home**, residence, dwelling, tent, habitation.' It was the dwelling place of God in all His glory. So God dwells in a 'home.'
Moses saw the complete fulness of the glory of God in Heaven, and received instructions from the Lord on how Israel should establish a tabernacle with all it's offerings, sacrifices and furniture, so that He should be able to dwell, live, and be at home in the midst of Israel

Exodus 24:10
"and they saw the God of Israel. And there was under His feet as it were a paved work of sapphire stone, and it was like the very heavens in its clarity."

Exodus 24:16 - Chapter 25:9
"Now the glory of the Lord rested on Mount Sinai, and the cloud covered it six days. And on the seventh day He called to Moses out of the midst of the cloud. The sight of the glory of the Lord was like a consuming fire on the top of the mountain in the eyes of the children of Israel. So Moses went into the midst of the cloud and went up into the mountain. And Moses was on the mountain forty days and forty nights. Then the Lord spoke to Moses, saying: "Speak to the children of Israel, that they bring Me an offering. From everyone who gives it willingly with his heart you shall take My offering. And this is the offering which you shall take from them: gold, silver, and bronze; blue, purple, and scarlet thread, fine linen, and goats' hair; ram skins dyed red, badger skins, and acacia wood; oil for the light, and spices for the anointing oil and for the sweet incense; onyx stones, and stones to be set in the ephod and in the breastplate. And let them make Me a sanctuary, that I may dwell among them. According to all that I show you, that is, the pattern of the tabernacle and the pattern of all its furnishings, just so you shall make it."

Moses came down the mountain and gave to those gifted to do the work, these same instructions on how to build the Tabernacle, along with all the instructions of it's activities and movements, according to what he had seen on the top of Mt. Sinai;

Exodus 31:1-11
"Then the Lord spoke to Moses, saying: "See, I have called by name Bezalel the son of Uri, the son of Hur, of the tribe of Judah. And I have filled him with the Spirit of God, in wisdom, in understanding, in knowledge, and in all manner of workmanship, to design artistic works, to work in gold, in silver, in bronze, in cutting jewels for setting, in carving wood, and to work in all manner of workmanship. "And I, indeed I, have appointed with him Aholiab the son of Ahisamach, of the tribe of Dan; and I have put wisdom in the

hearts of all the gifted artisans, that they may make all that I have commanded you: the tabernacle of meeting, the ark of the Testimony and the mercy seat that is on it, and all the furniture of the tabernacle— the table and its utensils, the pure gold lamp-stand with all its utensils, the altar of incense, the altar of burnt offering with all its utensils, and the laver and its base— the garments of ministry, the holy garments for Aaron the priest and the garments of his sons, to minister as priests, and the anointing oil and sweet incense for the holy place. According to all that I have commanded you they shall do."

Hebrews 8:5
"who serve the copy and shadow of the heavenly things, as Moses was divinely instructed when he was about to make the tabernacle. For He said, "See that you make all things according to the pattern shown you on the mountain."

Moses saw a heavenly vision of Jesus in all His glory. He then came down into the camp of Israel to establish an earthly expression of all he saw in Heaven. But the earthly tabernacle was simply a 'shadow' of the REAL tabernacle of God, who is Jesus Christ the King

Hebrews 8:1-2
"Now this is the main point of the things we are saying: We have such a High Priest, who is seated at the right hand of the throne of the Majesty in the heavens, a Minister of the sanctuary and of the **true tabernacle** *which the Lord erected, and not man."*

Hebrews 9:1-12
"Then indeed, even the first covenant had ordinances of divine service and the earthly sanctuary. For a tabernacle was prepared: the first part, in which was the lamp-stand, the table, and the showbread, which is called the sanctuary; and behind the second veil, the part of the tabernacle which is called the Holiest of All, which had the golden censer and the ark of the covenant overlaid on all sides with gold, in which were the golden pot that had the manna, Aaron's rod that budded, and the tablets of the covenant; and above it were the cherubim of glory overshadowing the mercy seat. Of these things we

cannot now speak in detail.

*Now when these things had been thus prepared, the priests always went into the first part of the tabernacle, performing the services. But into the second part the high priest went alone once a year, not without blood, which he offered for himself and for the people's sins committed in ignorance; the Holy Spirit indicating this, that the way into the Holiest of All was **not yet made manifest while the first tabernacle was still standing.** It was symbolic for the present time in which both gifts and sacrifices are offered which cannot make him who performed the service perfect in regard to the conscience—concerned only with foods and drinks, various washings, and fleshly ordinances imposed until the time of reformation.*

*But Christ came as High Priest of the good things to come, with **the greater and more perfect tabernacle not made with hands, that is, not of this creation.** Not with the blood of goats and calves, but with His own blood He entered the Most Holy Place once for all, having obtained eternal redemption."*

The Tabernacle of David

King David established a different tabernacle (home). It was a simple tent made of white linen, with no doors or sections divided by veils, as in the tabernacle of Moses. Moses' tabernacle had six pieces of furniture and could only be entered by priests who came from the tribe of Levi. Seven times a day the priests had to perform sacrifices and rituals, but David's new tabernacle was open for all to enter freely to worship, and had just one piece of furniture - the Ark of the Covenant (1 Chronicles 16:1). All sacrifices happened on the first day it opened and never happened again.

The Tabernacle of Moses had a veil hung between the Most Holy Place and the Holy Place. Only the High Priest, once a year, could enter into the Most Holy Place. But David's tabernacle had no such divide or veil. It spoke of a time when through the death and resurrection of Jesus Christ, the veil was to be removed forever and mans reconciliation to God was restored.

Matthew 27:50-51
"And Jesus cried out again with a loud voice, and yielded up His spirit. Then, behold, the veil of the temple was torn in two from top to bottom;"

Hebrews 10:19
"Therefore, brethren, having boldness to enter the Holiest by the blood of Jesus, by a new and living way which He consecrated for us, through the veil, that is, His flesh,"

David completely changed the tabernacle (home) from the structure and operation that Moses established. He knew there was coming a day when there would be no more need of any physical sacrifices, or for the veil that hung as a dividing wall in the tabernacle keeping us out from the full glory of God. So he built his tabernacle to reflect what he had prophetically seen. He 'saw' Jesus, the 'real' tabernacle of the glory of God, having given the greatest sacrifice of His blood and life to pay for all sin, for all time (Hebrews 7:26-27; Hebrews 9:12). David built the tent in Old Testament days, reflecting what he prophetically 'saw' would happen in the New Testament days, some 1000 years ahead of his day.

Only one piece of furniture was removed from the Tabernacle of Moses and placed into David's Tabernacle. It was the Ark of the Covenant, which represents the throne and rule of Christ the King.

So we see once again, the Vision, (the Ark of the Covenant and presence of God's glory), remained the same. But the Mission (the tabernacle structures, sacrifices and services) changed to reflect it was a new day, with a new revelation. The earthly tabernacles reflected and pointed to the One True Tabernacle and dwelling place of God - Jesus Christ.

The Temple of Solomon
David's son Solomon, built a Temple, a much larger and grandeur building, with many more pieces of furniture and restored the sacrificial system. But the Ark of the Covenant was still central in its layout. So the building, the earthly ministry (the Mission) is temporal and can change. But the eternal purpose (Vision of Jesus/the Ark of the Covenant, His presence and glory) does not change;

Hebrews 13:8
"Jesus Christ is the same yesterday, today, and forever."

It is ok to change the names and locations of buildings, times of gatherings, use new translations of the Bible, modern technology and equipment, as long as intimately knowing Jesus, establishing His heavenly Kingdom culture on earth and making Him known to all people everywhere, remains central to everything we do.

Jesus is eternal. But the way we reveal Him in the earth, is temporal and can change from nation to nation, culture to culture and generation to generation. The goal of Heaven's Vision never changes and we must endeavour to keep every follower of Christ totally focused on it. It is essential all leaders understand their function is to educate everyone under their oversight, to know what the eternal Vision of God really is and to spend their days living to achieve it.

The eternal Vision and plan of God is; **for every person to know Him, receive His heavenly culture, make Him known in every segment of our world, and make disciples of Jesus Christ** (Mk 16:15-16; Matt 28:18-20). God's desire is to reconcile the whole world to Himself, not establish an institution called 'The Church,' with it's hierarchy style of leadership and titles, built around religious rituals, regulations and rules.

Every Mission started, must be started for the purpose of reaching the yet unreached people in every segment of every nation, and to disciple those who turn to faith in Christ, into His likeness.

Question: Are you ready to change the model of Church, to realign it to a New Testament model so that this can begin to happen?

Chapter 2

Equip
Maximising Our Potential

Equip
Maximising Our Potential

A leader's role is not to do all the jobs in ministry, but to see they get done and done effectively, so that it brings great fruit for Jesus and the Kingdom of God. The best way to ensure this outcome is;

1. To equip every believer to have the same eternal **Vision**, which is to know Him personally and make Him known.

2. To equip every individual believer and enable them to fulfil their God-given **Mission**.

It is essential we equip every person to know Father intimately, and to be able to lead others to Christ and disciple them in such a way to reproduce the likeness of Christ. Multiplication is not only essential, but is the **only** way we can reach the whole world with the Gospel and disciple the nations, as commanded by Jesus.

Jesus had many disciples. After a night of prayer, Jesus chose 12 of them to be His apostles (Luke 6:12-17). After choosing them, He came down from the mountain with the 12 apostles and stood in the plains amongst a larger group of disciples and the multitude of people (v17). Paul the apostle had many disciples, to ensure the continual growth and expansion of the work of the Kingdom. He worked with them personally to train and prepare them for the task the Spirit had anointed and gifted them to do, and when ready, at the leading of the Spirit, he left them in a place to do it, entrusting them to the Holy Spirit (Titus 1:5; Acts 13:2-4; Acts 14:23). We must equip disciples of Jesus in this very same way.

Unleash The Hidden Potential
Within every believer there is unlimited reserves and resources deposited

by God, to achieve the task of establishing the Kingdom of God in every nation. This hidden potential within believers, remains mostly dormant in today's Church model, because we have adopted a model of Church that is not seen in the New Testament writings. We have veered off course from Gods blueprint, laid down by Jesus and the apostles. We have replaced it with man-made institutional preaching and teaching centres, where leaders have become more concerned with how many come into their building, not how many they equip and send out to expand the Kingdom. We have allowed the Church of Jesus Christ to become an organisation instead of a self-propelling organism, that simply reproduces and multiplies itself, invading and effecting every community and environment it enters.

The New Testament Church was explosive. It influenced culture so much that the leaders of those cultures felt threatened and therefore persecuted the Church to try to stop it's spread and influence. It was not organised and controlled by institutional leadership structures. It did not depend on leaders knowing or leading everything. It depended upon individuals receiving and obeying the Spirit's guiding, governing and grace alone (Acts 13:2-4; 14:23-28). This should be our pattern of leadership today.

When hundreds, or in some places thousands, of born again Spirit filled Christians, funnel into the same building each week of their lives, to watch the same few individuals do the 'ministry' every Sunday, being instructed when to come in, sit, stand, clap, give their offering and leave to go home until the next meeting, then we must see this is not successful Church, but actually the evidence of a man made religious system. My friend, it is not how many we have seated inside a building called 'Church,' but how many are actually equipped enough to go out, to fulfil their God given mission, is what determines if we are a 'successful' Kingdom-minded Church and leadership.

The Church of Jesus is not an institution or organisation, but a self-multiplying organism, that effectively spreads into every culture, bringing change to that culture until it is brought into alignment with the Kingdom of God. Therefore, it is imperative that we ensure every new believer understands they are not joining a club called 'Church,' but are signing up to become fully trained and equipped as a soldier in the army of God, to fight the fight of faith, in the greatest war on earth - the battle to see billions know and put their complete trust in Jesus Christ alone for their salvation.

Question: Which model of Church leadership do you operate? Is it time to change the model in order to fulfil His Vision?

Chapter 3

Encourage
The Gift Inside The Gift

Encourage
The Gift Inside The Gift

A New Priesthood

It is essential we help every believer in Christ to understand that **100% of the Church does 100% of the ministry.** The Old Testament writings reveal the segregation between the priesthood and the people. In the establishing of the Tabernacle of Moses, the Lord selects Levi's household to be the priestly order. The Levitical priests dressed in special robes, entered the Tabernacle building, handled the daily offerings and sacrifices, ministering to the Lord, whilst the people stood outside and watched. But the death and resurrection of Jesus changed everything and ushered in a new order. Just look at these verses from the New Testament writing;

> *"Therefore, holy brethren, **partakers of the heavenly calling**, consider the Apostle and **High Priest** of our confession, Christ Jesus." (Hebrews 3:1)*

> *"And having been perfected, He became the author of **eternal salvation** to all who obey Him, called by God as **High Priest** according to the order of Melchizedek," (Hebrews 5:9-10)*

Jesus Christ, God the Son, is now the eternal High Priest. Jesus was not born from the lineage of Levi but of the 'order of Melchizedek.' Therefore the 'order' has been changed;

> *"Therefore, if perfection were through the **Levitical** priesthood (for under it the people received the Law), what further need was there that another priest should rise according to the **order of Melchizedek,** and not be called according to the order of Aaron? For **the priesthood being changed**, of necessity there is also a*

*change of the law. For He of whom these things are spoken belongs to another tribe, from which no man has officiated at the altar. For it is evident that **our Lord arose from Judah**, of which tribe Moses spoke nothing concerning priesthood. And it is yet far more evident if, in the likeness of Melchizedek, **there arises another priest**, who has come, not according to the law of a fleshly commandment, but according to the power of an endless life. For He testifies; "You are a priest **forever** according to the **order of Melchizedek.**'" (Hebrews 7:11-17)*

*"Also there were many priests, because they were prevented by death from continuing, but He, because He continues forever, **has an unchangeable priesthood.**" (Hebrews 7:23-24)*

Because Jesus Christ is the eternal High Priest, He must therefore have an eternal priesthood, not born of man, but born of the Spirit;

*"But now He has obtained **a more excellent ministry,** in as much as He is also Mediator of a better covenant, which was established on better promises. For if that first covenant had been faultless, then no place would have been sought for a second........(v13) **In that He says, 'A new covenant,' He has made the first obsolete.'** " (Hebrews 8:6-7, 13)*

*"then He said, 'Behold I have come to do Your will, O God,' He **takes away the first that He may establish the second.** By that will **we have been sanctified** through the offering of the body of Jesus Christ once for all." (Hebrews10:9-10)*

Jesus Christ fulfilled the Old Covenant. It was not simply taken away and replaced. It had to be fulfilled because the Covenant had been established by God with man. Therefore God must fulfil His covenant. The birth, life, death, resurrection and ascension of Jesus entirely fulfilled God's first covenant. He was born as a man and born of God. He was both man and God in order for the Old Covenant to be fulfilled and the New One established.

He paid the price for mans sin by going to the cross in the place of Adam and Adam's lineage - all mankind. He became God's passover lamb who took on all sin, died and in His death took it all to the grave. Sin had been paid for. Then He rose again having defeated all sin and death to live the resurrection life and give unto every person the power to also live this new life.

In the upper room just before His death, Jesus introduced the New Covenant made between Himself and God the Father. The beneficiaries of this new covenant were all who were to believe in Him for everlasting life. These 'believers' would become His new order of an eternal priesthood;

> *"you also, as living stones, are being built up a **spiritual house**(hold), a **holy priesthood,** to offer up **spiritual** sacrifices acceptable to God through Jesus Christ.........v9 But you are a chosen generation, a **royal priesthood**, a holy nation, His own special people, that you may proclaim the praises of Him who called you out of darkness into His marvellous light." (1Peter 2:5, 9)*

We must see clearly, that through these verses the Lord is revealing the old order of priesthood, which was obtained by heritage from the earthly lineage of Levi, was ended, and changed entirely at the death, resurrection and ascension of Jesus. In it's place, Father ordained a new priestly order made up of every born-again believer in Christ.

Therefore, it is imperative that we in the Body of Christ, do not think lightly of this matter, but handle our placement and purpose, with great humility and care. **Every believer is called, sanctified and set apart for the purpose of priesthood.** Sharing your testimony, feeding the poor, counselling an individual, being a door-greeter or being a cell group leader are all the outworking of this new order of eternal priests. It is no longer confined to a few special people, with special titles and robes, leading meetings within special buildings. The people are the sanctuary and 'house' of God, the priesthood offering the offerings and the ones to do all the ministry.

The segregation of Priest and Laity, the special clothes, the special jobs, the special titles, the special places all connected to the ministry, have gone. They have been removed in Christ, and replaced with a new priesthood, who have been clothed in His robe of righteousness (Ephesians 4:24; Ephesians 6:14; Isaiah 61:10), whose sacrifices are their praises (Hebrews 13:15) who live a life of obedience to the will of God (Rom 12:1-2). Christ is now the Eternal High Priest of Heaven, and through Him, we have been given the priesthood of all believers. 100% of the priests are to do 100% of the ministry.

All can, and should be, being used by the Spirit to minister life wherever there is death, miracles wherever they find sickness and disease, and light wherever there is darkness. This New Testament priesthood needs no building, for their very lives are the living moving eternal Temple of God

> *"Or do you not know that **your body is the temple** of the Holy Spirit who is in you, whom you have from God," (1 Corinthians 6:19).*

They need no man-given titles, for they know they have been granted the greatest of all titles by God, who calls them His 'sons.' They need no altar or sacrifices of bulls and lambs to serve, for their lives and lips are their altar and sacrifice;

> *"I beseech you therefore, brethren, by the mercies of God, that you present your bodies a **living sacrifice**, holy, acceptable to God, which is your **reasonable service**." (Romans 12:1)*

> *"Therefore by Him let us continually offer the **sacrifice of praise to God, that is, the fruit of our lips, giving thanks** to His name." (Hebrews 13:15)*

This new priesthood of Christ, ministers His Life wherever they are, to whomever they meet

> *" For the law of the Spirit of life in Christ Jesus has made me free from the law of sin and death." (Romans 8:2)*

> *"who also made us **sufficient as ministers** of the new covenant, not of the letter but of the Spirit; for the letter kills, but the Spirit gives life." (2 Corinthians 3:6).*

They do not wait for people to come into a special building on a special day, at a special hour, to minister to them. They take the ministry of Christ out to wherever there are people, and do so every day of their lives, at any time day or night. This is the *'more excellent ministry'* mentioned in the Letter to the Hebrews (Hebrews 8:6).

When leading, teaching and training the congregation of God, we must view them, and speak to them **all** with great respect, treating them **all** with great dignity, because they are **all** a royal, kingly, priesthood. **All** are special to God and we must work with them, understanding they have been added to the Church by God Himself, for His glory and purpose. Our task is to receive them as such, and help uncover the deposit of 'heavenly gold' placed by God within each one.

A Miner of Divine Deposits
We must help every person to discover their calling, gifting's and mission. Our role is like a miner mining for gold. Miners labour to unearth a precious metal and bring it to the surface. The deposit of 'gold' was deposited by the Holy Spirit within every believer in Christ, the day they were truly born again;

> *"There are diversities of **gifts**, but the same Spirit. There are differences of **ministries**, but the same Lord. And there are diversities of **activities**, but it is the same God who works all in all. But the manifestation of the Spirit is given to each one for the profit of all:"* *(1Corinthians 12:4-7)*

> *"For I say, through the grace given to me, to everyone who is among you, not to think of himself more highly than he ought to think, but to think soberly, as God has dealt to **each one a measure of faith.** For as we have many members in one body, but all the members do not have the same function, so we, being many, are one body in Christ, and individually members of one another. Having then **gifts** differing according to the grace that is given to us, let us use them: if prophecy, let us prophesy in proportion to our faith; or **ministry**, let us use it in our ministering; he who teaches, in teaching; he who exhorts, in exhortation; he who gives, with liberality; he who leads, with diligence; he who shows mercy, with cheerfulness."* *(Romans 12:3-8).*

> *"But to each one of us **grace was given** according to the measure of*

*Christ's gift. Therefore He says:"When He ascended on high, He led captivity captive, and gave **gifts** to men."*

(Now this, "He ascended"—what does it mean but that He also first descended into the lower parts of the earth? He who descended is also the One who ascended far above all the heavens, that He might fill all things.)

And He Himself gave some to be apostles, some prophets, some evangelists, and some pastors and teachers, for the equipping of the saints for the work of ministry, for the edifying of the body of Christ, till we all come to the unity of the faith and of the knowledge of the Son of God, to a perfect man, to the measure of the stature of the fullness of Christ; that we should no longer be children, tossed to and fro and carried about with every wind of doctrine, by the trickery of men, in the cunning craftiness of deceitful plotting, but, speaking the truth in love, may grow up in all things into Him who is the head—Christ— from whom the whole body, joined and knit together by what every joint supplies, according to the effective working by which every part does its share, causes growth of the body for the edifying of itself in love." (Ephesians 4:7-16)

Mature Christians are gifted, anointed and called of God, and given the task to help every new believer bring this 'gold' deposited within them, to the surface, in order for them to release the hidden potential of Christ.

This deposit of 'gold' inside each believer, is God's gifting and purpose for their mission in life. They each have already received all the gifts, talents and anointing from the Lord to enable them to fulfil His mission on earth. It was deposited within them when they received the same Spirit that raised Christ from the dead (Romans 8:11).

It is our job to help each new believer become *'equipped'* by thoroughly understanding this new life they have received is the very life of Jesus. This new life affords them a new identity in Christ;

*"Therefore, if anyone is in Christ, he is a **new creation**; old things have passed away; behold, all things have become new." (2 Corinthians 5:17)*

"But as many as received Him, to them He gave the right to become **children of God**, *to those who believe in His name: who were born, not of blood, nor of the will of the flesh, nor of the will of man, but of God." (John 1:12-13)*

"For the earnest expectation of the creation eagerly waits for the revealing of the **sons of God***. For the creation was subjected to futility, not willingly, but because of Him who subjected it in hope; because the creation itself also will be delivered from the bondage of corruption into the glorious liberty of the* **children of God***." (Romans 8:19-21)*

"For you are all **sons of God** *through faith in Christ Jesus. For as many of you as were baptised into Christ* **have put on Christ***. There is neither Jew nor Greek, there is neither slave nor free, there is neither male nor female; for you are all one in Christ Jesus. And if you are Christ's, then* **you are Abraham's seed, and heirs according to the promise***." (Galatians 3:26-29)*

"And because you are **sons***, God has sent forth the Spirit of His Son into your hearts, crying out, "Abba, Father!" Therefore you are no longer a slave but* **a son, and if a son, then an heir of God through Christ***." (Galatians 4:6-7)*

They are no longer to be named 'sinners,' but 'sons' and sons of God. They have been given a new DNA, the very nature of God Himself, because they are born of His 'seed.' They have His righteousness, holiness, faith, power and authority and are no longer enslaved to sin and death, but in Christ have been given His eternal life. They are joint-heirs with Christ right now, not sometime in the future when they are in heaven. They rule and reign in life as does Christ.

It is imperative that we help every believer understand that this 'new life' within them is the very life of God, in order to release this 'gold' deposit of God from within them, into the earth. It is not our job to tell people what their function and purpose is. It is our job to encourage the individual to discover and uncover what it is. The mission comes from within their spirit.

Parents raise children to have the capability and confidence to do life. When the child is first born, the parent does everything for them. But we do not continue this practice for the rest of their lives. From the very beginning we use every moment and method to teach the child to do everything for themselves. The older they get, the more you have to teach them to do things for themselves and to be responsible for their decisions and actions. We teach them that the older they become, the more they must contribute in every way, into the home and family life, in preparation for their own future. Everything we train them to do is for one purpose - to leave home and reproduce their own family and home life. We equip them to follow the blueprint of establishing and filling the earth with self-multiplying and self-propelling 'family' units. This is an eternal blueprint established by God in the beginning;

> *Genesis 1:28*
> *"Then God blessed them, and God said to them, "Be fruitful and multiply; fill the earth and subdue it; have dominion over the fish of the sea, over the birds of the air, and over every living thing that moves on the earth."*

Everything God creates, He creates it to reproduce and multiply. When you are born-again you are born 'of God.' Therefore He has given you the ability to multiply. A Christian reproduces the life of God in others.

Every person multiplying is God's blueprint from the beginning. Then why have we gone away from this pattern when doing 'Church?' We must return to His blueprint to see the unlimited potential of God released through every one of His sons.

Children or Sons?

To equip means to enable every individual to read the Word to learn, to hear God, to walk obediently with Him and teach others to do likewise, all by themselves. When we have done this with every 'child' of God, only then have we made a disciple, and a true disciple is one who has become a 'son' of God.

It is easier and quicker to give birth to a child, than to raise it to become a mature and responsible adult. It is the same within the Kingdom of God. A person can come to faith in Christ in a moment. But to disciple them sometimes takes years, with many issues to work through and resolve in their lives.

Disciples - Carbon Copies of The Master

True discipleship is more than just evangelism. Jesus did not tell us to evangelise the nations. He commanded us to make disciples of all who come in faith to Christ;

> *Matthew 28:19*
> *"Go therefore and make disciples of all the nations, baptising them in the name of the Father and of the Son and of the Holy Spirit, teaching them to observe all things that I have commanded you; and lo, I am with you always, even to the end of the age." Amen."*

Let us stop just seeking for 'converts,' or people to say a quick 'prayer of salvation' in our evangelistic endeavours. Let us start with the end in mind. Let those we lead to Christ understand, before they make their decision to accept Jesus Christ as their Lord and Saviour, that they are making a life-long decision to become His disciple.

The word 'disciple' means a 'carbon copy of the master, in every way.' It does not mean to be his 'apprentice' to learn some skills. It means that when the process of discipleship is completed, then the disciple has the same motives, thought patterns, attitudes, goals, purpose, attributes and lifestyle as the Master, as well as His 'skills.' Is this not what Paul means when writing:

> *"I beseech you therefore, brethren, by the mercies of God, that you present your bodies a living sacrifice, holy, acceptable to God, which is your reasonable service. And do not be conformed to this world, but be transformed by the renewing of your mind, that you may prove what is that good and acceptable and perfect will of God." (Romans 12:1-2).*

Chapter 4

Evaluate
It's How You Finish

Evaluate
It's How You Finish

It's not how you start, but how you finish that is important. We cannot just be concerned if someone can start their God-given Mission, but whether they have the ability to finish what they start. The work Jesus has called us to participate with Him in is like a marathon, not a short sprint. The Vision of Heaven is eternal, and the Mission He calls each person to finish will occupy them for the rest of their earthly life. So, we must equip them to do so, with ever increasing faith and fruitfulness.

At the time of writing this book the youngest girl ever to give birth was just 5.7 years old. Are you shocked? I was when discovering this fact. The father of the child was just over 7 years old. This shows how young you can be to reproduce a child. The issue is not just whether someone can impregnate or give birth to a child, but whether they are capable and mature enough to be a good parent. These children now needed a support network around them to enable them to parent their child.

This same principle is seen in bringing someone to salvation through Christ. Every follower of Jesus has the ability to lead someone else to Christ within days of their own experience of salvation. But do they personally yet really know Jesus for themselves, or truly understand what the gospel of Jesus really is? Therefore, training and support must be given to every new believer in Christ, in order to grow quickly, because when they are still newly converted to Christ, they can be at the most 'contagious' time of their spiritual walk with Jesus and want to tell everyone about what has happened to them. Every new believer has approximately thirty close unsaved family members and friends. We must work with them tirelessly at this point, not to miss the opportunity to reach through them into their network of unsaved family and friends, who will probably be very open to listening to their encounter with Christ.

Sadly, it is at this point that normal Church protocol makes a big mistake. Instead of reaching through this new believer in order to engage with their unsaved family and friends, the Church instead draws the newly saved individual into the Church system, and thereby disconnects them from the very group they can influence the most. We bring them into the Church institution instead of the Church entering into their family and friends network to lead even more to salvation in Christ, and establish the kingdom of God amongst a new peoples group.

A New Idea?

I remember the day my son Matthew, and his wife Becci, brought home their new born son Jesse. They came into my home and placed him into my arms so I could enjoy some time with him. After a little while it was time for them to leave. It was as I handed Jesse back to them, and they left for their own home, that I realised a shocking, profound, yet simple spiritual truth that had been eroded from Church lifestyle. Matt and Becci took Jesse with them. They did not leave him in my house for me to raise him. **They birthed him, therefore they would raise him.** It was so clear to me. As parents, we had raised our son Matthew with the necessary abilities to have his own family. He and Becci had the ability to birth and raise their own children. They did not leave Jesse with us to raise him - which sadly, is the method of most churches.

In most expressions of today's Church, the congregation is encouraged to bring unsaved people to Church services, in order for them to hear the pastor, or preacher, communicate the gospel of Jesus. At the end of the message the individual is invited to accept Jesus as their Lord and Saviour, and therefore become born again. Many do so.

Immediately after the service, these new 'babies' in Christ, are taken off to another room to be prayed for by strangers. They are given some literature and encouraged to attend the 'New Believers' class, which means they are placed into the care of another different person in the Church that they have never met, to begin the process of being a Christian and active Church Member. This one small error causes the whole Church to become out of alignment with the blueprint laid down by Father, from the very beginning.

This Church procedure may seem harmless, but it sends to the wider congregation of believers the message that they are not capable to do this task. It needs to be stopped immediately and replaced by us believing that if a person can witness and bring someone to the point of salvation, then they can do the whole job of discipling them from the beginning. They should be included in the process, in order to learn effective ways of discipling new believers.

The pattern of God, revealed from the beginning, must be restored;

> *"then God blessed **them**, and God said to **them**, 'Be fruitful and multiply; fill the whole earth.....' " (Genesis 1:28)*

This blessing to multiply was upon **all** mankind, not just Adam. The command to multiply in order to fill the earth, is a perpetual command, for every person, in every nation, throughout the generations. In fact, the first pages of Genesis show clearly that everything God creates has life within itself to reproduce and be fruitful. Therefore, every new believer is blessed by God to reproduce new believers. Sheep produce sheep.

This command and blessing is not just for evangelists, pastors, leaders or 'special' people in the Church. It is for us all. The whole of your natural body is made up from cells multiplying and passing life onto each other, so that your body can grow, be healthy, operate at full capacity and multiply itself. Every individual cell is given this responsibility by Father. The natural body points clearly to the spiritual Body of Christ;

> *1 Corinthians 15:46*
> *"However, the spiritual is not first, but the natural, and afterward the spiritual."*

It is essential we retrain every individual born again Christian, to personally lead individuals to Christ, baptise them, and disciple them. If we do this one thing, then the Church will explode with life. Why? Because the life contained within the **whole** body of Christ, not just the few 'anointed' ones in the Church system, is being released to fulfil the call of God to disciple the nations. Every new baby that is born releases great joy in the family. Imagine the joy released in the Church, when all around us, every member of the Church is bringing new people to Christ, throughout the year.

When we don't use God's method of personal discipleship, then we take away from the whole congregation, the most natural thing in God's creation. We take away their joy of becoming spiritual 'parents,' and having their own spiritual family unit. This true personal discipleship method must be restored and remain the opportunity and joy for all His disciples, in order for the most incredible ability of multiplication to be released in the earth. Every believer has the ability to lead someone to Christ and disciple them, not just the pastor or evangelist.

> *"And He Himself gave some to be apostles, some prophets, some evangelists and some pastors and teachers, for the **equipping of the saints** for the work of ministry, for the **edifying of the body of Christ**, till we **all** come to a unity of the faith and of the knowledge of the Son of God, to a perfect man, to the measure of the stature of the fullness of Christ, that we should **no longer be children**......"* (Ephesians 4:11-14)

Sons of God

These few verses in the Letter to the Ephesian Church, reveal to us clearly the role of the five-fold ministry. It is not to do all the ministry, but to help everyone else in the body of Christ grow and be the ministers of the gospel of Jesus, and to become mature sons, not remain as spiritual children. The one thing that causes children to grow up is to prepare them and then give them responsibilities in life. When this is not the process in a family, then the child grows to be older, but not mature. God has no desire for His children to remain immature children. He wants us to grow and become like Him.

> *"But as many as received Him, to them He gave the right to become children (Teknon) of God."* (John 1:12)

> *"For as many as are led by the Spirit of God, these are the sons (Huios) of God.........For the earnest expectation of creation eagerly waits for the revealing of the sons (Huios) of God."* (Romans 8:14,19)

In these two quotes from the Bible, we see John, when referring to becoming a disciple of Jesus and a child of God, he uses the Greek word 'Teknon,' which literally means 'born of.' While Paul in his letter to the Christians in Rome, uses an entirely different Greek word, which is '*Huios,*' meaning 'son of.' One word speaks of the birth of a child and the other the process of becoming 'like daddy.' There is a vast difference between the two. Each believer must not just chose to be born again, but must also desire to mature in Christ, and must be given the opportunity to do so.

When the pattern of Church adopted is based upon the concept that Church happens in meetings inside a building that has a stage, and on it each week the same few 'ministers' lead us and instruct us, then the opportunity to truly grow and see the Holy Spirit grace within every believer flow through them, is almost impossible. The majority of people, in this model of Church, just sit and receive. This model operates on the understanding that the Church is all about the size of the congregation that attends, not upon God's purpose for every child to grow and multiply. It keeps believers as 'children,' instead of raising everyone as 'sons' of God.

If instead, we grasp and teach that the Church is a spiritual family unit that meets in, and flows from homes, then suddenly there comes an explosion, a new liberty and freedom. Instead of all the ministry operating in one building, with a small group of people doing the ministry, it leaps to hundreds of discipleship cells right across the city or region. Immediately the pastoral work is no longer done by one leader, but is released to individuals or couples who have gathered a small flock into their home, in order to disciple them. This pattern means all gifts and ministries are multiplied, and the majority of believers can now exercise their gifts and ministries, instead of the few.

Implementing the discipleship cell concept of Church, releases the Holy Spirit to reveal His gifting and ministry in and through a limitless group of individuals. The purpose of every discipleship cell is to raise up equipped disciples and send them out to reproduce the cell - the family unit! Instruction happens in large auditorium styled Church meetings. But you cannot disciple anyone from a platform. True discipleship is all about the accountability you experience from personal heart to heart relationships seen in great families. So many Churches today experience new visitors each Sunday, but also experience that they cannot keep them. This is because meetings can attract individuals, but it is true relationships that give people significance, security and meaning. When Father said in the very beginning, *"It is not good for man to be alone, I will make Him a helper comparable to him."* (Genesis 2:18) He wasn't meaning Adam needed a crowd around him to help him do the work. He meant Adam needed a wife and family to co-exist with and do life. Adam needed a marriage and family unit.

I travel all over the world and get to minister in wonderful places, see wonderful cities, mountains or oceans, and have had the privilege to minister in both large and small meetings. These experiences have affected me greatly over the years and I have appreciated the joy it has given me. But none of these places can ever come close to giving me the joy I get when at home with my family. Every believer needs a spiritual 'home.' A group of individuals who have been forged by God into a family who worship, pray and do life together, and give of themselves to help every individual grow in Christ and become all that Father intended.

It is time to evaluate Church process in light of all I have just written. Are you actively implementing the organic process of raising 'sons' of God? Are you releasing the whole Church to do the whole ministry? Are you equipping people to be genuine disciplers, not just Church attenders? If you are, then I commend you, for you are rare indeed. If you are not, then what is your desire or plan? To continue doing something that produces little fruit, or to achieve the goal of Christ? Are you willing to take a risk and implement a new idea, which is not new at all?

Chapter 5

Engage
Beginning Their Journey

Engage
Beginning Their Journey

Leadership has a purpose. It is to ensure every person actually engages into their God-given Mission, in order to fulfil the Vision;

> *"Train up a child in the way he should go, and when he is old he will not depart from it." (Proverbs 22:6)*

> *"To everything there is a season, a time for every purpose under Heaven." (Ecclesiastes 3:1)*

Everything created or started by God, has His purpose already fashioned into it. It is the purpose of parents (natural and spiritual), and all leadership, to help each individual discover His purpose, which will be their guide for the rest of their life's journey. Glimpses of the purpose of God can be seen from the earliest years of a child. It 'leaks' out in very natural ways.

In my own personal life I can remember my mother telling me that as a very small child I was fascinated by suitcases. Apparently I couldn't walk past a shop displaying them. She told me that I would cry and make a scene until she let me go into the shop and touch the suitcases. On one such occasion my mother turned to my father and said of me, "this boy is born to travel." She was right. I have spent my Christian life going to the nations taking the message of Jesus physically into over 50 nations and through our literature and our TV programs into over 155 nations. Our desire is too take the gospel of Jesus and the message of true reformation, to all 195 nations presently on this planet. So, I guess my mother was right!

When first born every baby already has within them the ability to walk. They just need time to grow, learn balance, gain strength and then they will walk by themselves, beginning with such small steps, encouraged and aided by others who already walk. We are not giving them the ability to walk. This is already built into the DNA of their body. All we are doing is aiding what is already within them to come to the surface. This is exactly our role in helping all new babies in Christ.

When a baby is still within the womb, the parents already know, and are excited, that their child will one day walk. They know it, because it is the way of life since Cain was born (Genesis 4:1). Inside the womb the baby is learning to move it's limbs. As it's life unfolds, so the baby discovers what it can do, and loving parents are just aiding this discovery process and helping their child handle and use every one of their discoveries. This same principle operates in the development of spiritual children of God. We must simply aid them, knowing that Father has already placed within them His purpose, and every talent, gift and anointing to achieve it.

The Purpose of Revelation

> *"Where there is no* **revelation***, the people cast off* **restraint***, but happy is he who keeps the law."* *(Proverbs 29:18)*

> *"Write the* **vision** *(revelation) and* **make it plain** *on* **tablets***, that he may* **run** *who reads it."* *(Habakkuk 2:2)*

The purpose of receiving revelation from the Lord, is to enable everyone to know for certainty their purpose in life, to be able to communicate it clearly and concisely, and for the revelation to act as blinkers, keeping them focused on fulfilling it.

These two verses from the Bible contain some important keys to helping people fulfil their God-given Mission;

1. God has a purpose for everyone. Everyone who is born into this life has purpose. The person themselves may never know this, but it is still the truth. It is a tragedy for a person to be born, and live their whole life not knowing why they even lived. If someone is unaware that there is a purpose for their life, gifting, talent or ability, then they will either abuse it, mis-use it, or never ever fully use it for its

correct purpose. To live life on purpose is absolutely essential to every human being. It will give them satisfaction, significance and sight (direction). There is nothing more soul destroying than for a person to spend their entire daily life doing something their heart has no passion for, or that they are not gifted to do.

2. The wording *'the people cast off restraint'* means they 'perish, go backwards, dismiss.' The writer is trying to communicate that the revelation acts in such a way as to keep you moving forward and on track. Without knowing this revelation, then a person lives aimlessly, because they have no target or goal to aim for. It is the target that causes the arrow to be aimed and fired. Without the target then the bow and arrow is aimless and its ability never released. It is the target, the goal, the purpose, that gives the arrow (the person's life) direction. The revelation of your purpose (Vision & Mission) keeps you living every day making the right decisions on what, or what not to do, in order to hit the target and reach the goal and the prize;

> *Philippians 3:12-16*
> *"Not that I have already attained, or am already perfected; but I press on, that I may lay hold of that for which Christ Jesus has also laid hold of me. Brethren, I do not count myself to have apprehended; but one thing I do, forgetting those things which are behind and reaching forward to those things which are ahead, **I press toward the goal for the prize of the upward call of God in Christ Jesus**.*
> *Therefore let us, as many as are mature, have this mind; and if in anything you think otherwise, God will reveal even this to you. Nevertheless, to the degree that we have already attained, let us walk by the same rule, let us be of the same mind."*

3. Proverbs 29 declares that if we keep to the law of the vision/mission, then we will be happy. Knowing and accepting God's purpose for your life, and daily working it out, releases within you a deep contentment and joy. Why? Because stress comes from not knowing what to do or which way to go. Once you absolutely know Father's purpose for your life, it removes the stress in decision making,

because once you know your purpose and His direction, you also automatically know what it isn't. Therefore, many decisions in life are automatically taken care of. You know when to say 'no.' You'll have a freedom to say 'no' to anything and everything that doesn't help you fulfil His purpose.

4. If a person cannot communicate to me within 1 minute what God's purpose and mission is for their life, then I know immediately that they still don't know what it is. Habakkuk tells us to *"write the revelation and make it plain."* If a person cannot write it down clearly and swiftly, then they will not be able to speak it out clearly and swiftly, because they really do not know what it is yet. But when they really know and understand the revelation of God's purpose for their life, then they are focused and consumed by it and communicate it with passion and clarity.

5. Habakkuk says that when people read the revelation that is written down, *"he may run."* This implies two things. Speed and direction. It says men will run. Thats speed. When people have no purpose in life, they seem to just meander through life, existing and bouncing from one situation to another. But knowing purpose gives you a drive and a passion to fulfil it, because you know it is the very reason you came into this life. Habakkuk does not say which way the runner will run. Some will run hastily away from the Vision/Mission, whilst others will run hastily towards it. When you know and accept your God-given Mission in life, you will be so consumed and passionate about it, that it will cause two people groups to react. One group will distance themselves from you, whilst the other group will be drawn closer to you. The one group distancing from you are those who do not have the same Vision/Mission as you. The other group are the ones drawn to you because they have the same, or similar Vision/Mission as yourself, or are the ones the Holy Spirit is drawing to you, to help you achieve it.

6. Finally, Habakkuk instructs that when we communicate the Vision/Mission, we should *'make it plain.'* This means to make it clear and simple to understand or grasp. In other words the Vision/Mission is simple, not complicated. To know Jesus and make Him known to all

people is plain, clear and simple to grasp. There is no confusion in it and anyone can understand it and respond to it. This is the very basic understanding of God's purpose for everyone's life. Let's not make it complicated for them to grasp.

It is so sad watching people in life trying to live either not knowing their purpose, or for some reason knowing it, but never being given the chance to achieve it. I know that individual will never find what they are looking for in life, because everything we dream and hope for in life, is somehow attached to knowing Father and living to achieve His purpose for our life. They are connected.

In 2006 the Lord broke in on my life and showed me His plan for me, for the rest of my life. Here it is:

1. To reach and disciple one leader and one believer in every nation of this world, every year, giving them the resources to repeat this process.

2. To raise up a generation of worshippers.

3. To raise up and international network of 1 Million Homes Of Praise & Evangelism (inH.O.P.E), which will operate as personal worship and discipleship centres.

4. To bring a true radical reformation to the way we do Church and return the Church back to the New Testament model and mode of operation.

Being Determines Doing!

The ultimate Vision of God is to transform everyone into the likeness of His Son Jesus Christ. And He achieves this through the very Mission He gives to each of us. It is the journey from beginning to end that forces us to learn to draw closer to Him in order to achieve it. Our closeness to Him is His ultimate desire. It is this closeness that enables us to effectively fulfil the Mission for our lives. Intimacy with Father is the foundational key to every fulfilled life. Being intimate with Him is more important than doing something for Him, because in the place of intimacy with Him you discover your true identity and relationship with Him. Your identity determines the way you believe and live out your life.

Great leaders know that within every born again believer, dwells the life and ability of God, and therefore spend their time and effort in nurturing individuals to know Father more intimately, to know their true identity in Christ perfectly, and to know and engage in God's purpose for their life, giving them all the necessary support needed to accomplish it.

Chapter 6

Eliminate

20/20 Vision

Eliminate
20/20 Vision

Teaching people to 'prune' their lives of the things that distract them from their God-given Mission (even good Church things) is essential, if we desire to see them achieve God's plan for their life.

When we enter Heaven and are greeted by Jesus, He will not ask us how many people attended our meetings, were members of our Churches, how many books, dvd's or cd's of our teaching we sold, nor how many departments or staff we had in our organisation. But He will ask us about our fruitfulness!

Mark 4:18-20
"Now these are the ones sown among thorns; they are the ones who hear the word, and the cares of this world, the deceitfulness of riches, and the desires for other things entering in choke the word, and it becomes **unfruitful***. But these are the ones sown on good ground, those who hear the word, accept it, and* **bear fruit***: some thirtyfold, some sixty, and some a hundred."*

John 15:5-8
"I am the vine, you are the branches. He who abides in Me, and I in him, bears **much fruit***; for without Me you can do nothing. If anyone does not abide in Me, he is cast out as a branch and is withered; and they gather them and throw them into the fire, and they are burned. If you abide in Me, and My words abide in you, you will ask what you desire, and it shall be done for you. By this My Father is glorified, that you bear* **much fruit***; so you will be My disciples."*

Colossians 1:10
*"that you may walk worthy of the Lord, fully pleasing Him, being **fruitful** in every good work and increasing in the knowledge of God;*

It is not busyness (foliage) that Jesus is looking for, but actual fruit, which is the evidence that His life within someone has multiplied itself through them.

Father sows the 'seed,' which is the Word of God, into the heart of anyone who in faith repents of living their life in disobedience to Him, and turns and puts their entire faith in Jesus as their Saviour. The seed, which is the seed of His life and nature, embeds itself in a persons spirit, takes root and grows. The parable of the sower (Mark 4:18-20; Luke 8:11-15) reveals that the individual must 'keep' or 'hold onto' the seed and not let it become chocked with thorns and thistles in life, making the seed become less fruitful, or not fruitful at all. Notice, in this parable it is explained it is the 'cares of this world' or the 'desire for other things' that chokes the seed. It is the temporal and earthly things that can make the eternal things unfruitful.

Disciples of Jesus produce disciples of Jesus, not departments or projects. They are meant to re-produce the life of Jesus, not the life of the project of a institution or organisation. The focus and heartbeat of every believer in the Kingdom of God, must be to share their love of Jesus, not just in actions, but also in words. For it is the words of the Gospel of Jesus, that create faith in other people causing them to believe in Jesus and begin the journey of being one of His disciples.

We can often fall into the trap of being more concerned about how many people we can get into the building each week, and how many we can train to become committed members and workers in the Church, rather becoming fruitful disciples able to lead others to Christ through sharing their faith in Him.
Our focus should never be on how many people we can get in and keep, but how many are being sent out, fully equipped and energised to accomplish their God-given Mission, which is to be fruitful disciples.

Have you noticed the Kingdom of God is an upside down Kingdom? The way up (promotion) is achieved by going down (demotion of self by promotion of Christ);

John 12:23-25
"The hour has come when the Son of Man must be glorified. Most assuredly, I say to you, unless a grain of wheat falls to the ground and dies, it remains alone; but if it dies, it produces much grain (fruit). He who loves his life will lose it, and he who hates his life in this world will keep it for eternal life."

Jesus is saying, the key for success in God's Kingdom is that if you desire to have a true life, then die and if you wish to keep, then give away! This is the complete opposite lifestyle to the kingdoms of this world. Leaders need to learn to 'loose' His people to fulfil their God-given Mission, in order for the Lord to draw more people in. If we seek to release more people, the Lord will bring more people in to be equipped, because He sees our focus is in alignment to the assignment of His Kingdom. It is a spiritual law in operation;

Luke 6:38
"Give, and it will be given to you: good measure, pressed down, shaken together, and running over will be put into your bosom. For with the same measure that you use, it will be measured back to you."

Unharness The People
It is better for us to have one purpose and achieve it well, than try to be responsible for five things, and do them all to an average level. An experiment was once done with horses that confirms this principle.

A large horse was harnessed to a heavily ladened cart and the horse pulled it. That same horse was harnessed to five carts each weighing 20% of the original total weight, but the horse could not pull the carts, even though it was the exact same total weight. The only difference being five harnessed loads instead of one. People react this same way. Too many responsibilities pulling on us, cause individuals to lose focus and instead of single focus, they have to be multi-focused.

The english word 'division,' is derived from an old French word which means to separate the one thing into two or more things. Great eyesight is called 20/20 vision, meaning each eye has the same perfect strength and focus. Even though you have two eyes they operate in such a way as if you had just one eye. When your eyes do not operate this way, then you get what is called 'double-vision,' which means the one has become two. Instead of seeing one picture, you actually see two, because your eyes are not focusing as perfectly as they could. Our clear Vision deteriorates into a blurred focus. We must be restored to the place we see clearly our Mission and have no other focus to distract us from it.

This is why it is essential that we all learn to know our God-given Mission in life. Then we can eliminate everything that tries to pull us in different directions - even if it is only slightly different to our real Mission. We must learn to get our focus right.

The Purpose Of Pruning

When I grew up as a young boy in Wales, I would watch my father working in the garden and be mesmerised by how he pruned bushes or trees. I once remember watching him prune a rose bush and asked him if he could teach me how to do it. He taught me where on each branch to prune and why it was to be pruned in that precise place. Then he handed me the secateurs, and pointed out where he wanted me to cut the branch of the rose bush. I was shocked. The bush was taller than me and he wanted me to cut the branch right down to where almost nothing was left of the branch.
He saw my reaction and simply encouraged me by telling me the bush would have an even longer branch with more flowers the following year. But it seemed to me, such a drastic cutback.

My father then explained why the process of pruning actually helped the bush grow stronger and higher, bearing more flowers the following year, even after being pruned so harshly. He showed me how some branches looked really good, had lots of leaves, but had very few flowers on them, while other branches had much more flowers on them. He was cutting away all the poor flowering (unfruitful) branches, because they diverted the life and strength of the bush from the branches that were bearing more flowers (more fruitful). Therefore, the energy of the plant was focussed on less branches in order to make them produce more flowers/fruit. I had no idea at the time, that he was teaching me a powerful principle seen in the New

Testament and one I have implemented in my life for over 40 years;

> *"I am the true vine and My Father is the vinedresser. Every branch in Me that does not bear fruit He takes away; and every branch that bears fruit He prunes, **that it may bear more fruit.**" (John 15:2)*

Let me repeat a principle because it is so vital to life and ministry.

> *"**The purpose of removing and pruning the branches is to allow the strength and life of the plant to flow to less branches, in order for the remaining ones to bear more fruit.**"*

In fact, Jesus states that it is Fathers great desire that we bear **much** fruit, and that bearing much fruit will bring us personal joy (John 15:8, 11,16). Therefore we must expect Him to deal with us this same way. I believe that at this time in history, the Holy Spirit is bringing a true reformation to our understanding of Church and ministry. It will cause many to put down the many unfruitful activities they have been doing, to focus and achieve fruitfulness in the one thing Jesus gave them to do. Many within the institution of Church will call these individuals unfaithful, disloyal and uncommitted, when the truth is the very opposite. They are becoming more faithful and loyal to Jesus and His plan and focus for their life. We are not called to be loyal and faithful to an institution, but to Jesus.

Dear friend, carrying too much, or too many responsibilities and work-loads, will burden and distract you from your God-given purpose. Especially when much of what you have to do is not what you are called or gifted of God to do. You will lose your joy and be unable to bear the measure of fruit Father has always wanted you to produce. Prune your responsibilities and focus, by removing those things that distract you from the one thing that fulfils your Mission and purpose in life. Then you will be able to help those around you do likewise.

Chapter 7

Empower
Delegate His Authority

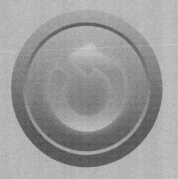

Empower
Delegate His Authority

A parent that delegates authority to their children, will raise mature children. A persons age does not guarantee their maturity. Being able to handle responsibilities correctly does. Great parents understand and apply this principle in their active role in raising their sons and daughters.

A parent has authority in their child's life. That authority is not given to them to dictate, but to instruct and protect their child. In the child's early years, it is necessary for parents to use that authority over all the child's life because the child is unable to care for itself. But it is not meant to remain this way. Good parents raise a child to understand and accept the responsibility for their own life. As they grow we teach them to do everything for themselves, even learning to make the right choices.

A parent has authority in a child's life to the measure they have responsibility for the child. The more the child matures to take responsibility for themselves, the less authority a parent needs to use on behalf of their child. The purpose of parenting is to raise the child into a mature adult, who has accepted and learnt how to handle that authority, and has taken responsibility for their lives. As the child grows, and the authority lessens on the parent and increases on the child, a new dynamic must be learnt by both parents and the child. The parent must learn to take the role of oversight and support, and the child must learn to take responsibility and learn to be thankful to their parents and honour them;

Exodus 20:12
"Honour your father and your mother, that your days may be long upon the land which the Lord your God is giving you."

The word 'honour' means; 'to make glorious and boast of.' It conveys the understanding meaning to esteem, think highly of, boast, speak in a manner that honours them privately and publicly. No parent is perfect. But, every parent must raise and train their child, in such manner, that the child can grow up honouring them. A child must grow up understanding their parents cannot be perfect, any more than they, the child, can be a perfect son or daughter. You can honour an imperfect parent, but not an abusive, dictatorial or uncaring one.

Parents are not the owners of their children. They are the stewards of their upbringing and early years. As stewards we understand our children belong to another - Jesus Christ. He is the author of their life and it is to Him we eventually give an account for what we have done with our life. When we believe we are the owner of something then we can have the attitude that we can do whatever we want with it, because it is our possession. When we understand something is not ours, but given to us to take care of by Jesus, then our whole attitude towards our role changes drastically.

Church leaders are not the parents of the people of God. Our heavenly Father is their father. Therefore we are to be the stewards of His people. They belong to Him. They are not our possession to do whatever we want. As said in an earlier chapter, we are to honour them and treat them all with dignity, for they belong to Him.

Knowing we are but stewards changes our perspective and mode of operation as leaders. We do not have authority over them, but authority to nurture and oversee in order to guide and protect them.

A Kingdom Of Sons

Great leaders, in the Body of Christ, understand and operate this same principle, when it comes to an individuals spiritual growth, because they know a leaders role is to develop 'sons' of God, not keep them as 'children' of God. People may begin as children, but we must help them grow into sons.

Every child of God is granted the full authority of Jesus Christ when they are first born again. But they do not understand what this means, and are therefore unable to operate in its fullness. It is the task of all leadership to help them spiritually mature in their understanding and handling of the fulness of the authority of Jesus Christ, for themselves.

We need to grasp and understand one simple, but serious, truth. *No disciple of Jesus Christ needs permission to do what the Holy Spirit has told them to do.* They may need someone's help and wisdom, but not their permission. The Lord has already granted the person the authority to do whatever He told them to do. The function of a leader or spiritual parent, is to empower every disciple to live in such a way that brings honour to Jesus, obtain the wisdom of God to handle the great authority He has invested in them, and at the same time, honour their leaders or spiritual parent(s).

We are granted the authority, wisdom and the grace of Jesus, to help individuals grow up in Christ. Sometimes in the areas of ministry and church meetings, we may need to exercise spiritual authority to keep order in the meetings, or in the work of the ministry (1 Corinthians 14:40), but this does not mean we have **all** authority over the individuals personal, marriage, family or ministry life. We have authority to speak, teach, instruct in the things of God, but not rule as some earthly dictator over their entire life.

God never takes away our personal authority or will. He slowly teaches us over the years to submit to His wisdom and direction. He teaches each person truth, so that the individual can grow and mature in the truth, to live in the authority He gave them. This must be the way all leaders and spiritual parents operate in His Kingdom.

> *"**All** authority has been given unto Me, in Heaven and on earth."*
> *(Matt 28:18)*

If Jesus has **ALL** authority, then you and I have none! We operate in His delegated authority, not our own. He is the only King in the Kingdom of God. We are not to operate as if everyone and everything in ministry is under our authority. It is not. Everything is, and must remain, under the authority of Jesus. This protects leaders from ever being tempted to usurp His authority the way Lucifer (the Devil) did.

All delegated authority given by Jesus, is given for a purpose;

> *"All authority has been given unto Me in Heaven and on earth.*
> *Go therefore, and make disciples of all nations, baptising them*

in the Name of the Father and of the Son and of the Holy Spirit,
teaching them to observe all things that I have commanded you;"
(Matt 28:18-20)

Did you see that? Jesus has total authority in all realms and the moment He reveals this truth to the apostles, He links it to the purpose of discipling every nation into the same truths He has taught the apostles. He gives His authority to leaders and spiritual parents to get this task done, by raising and releasing sons of the Father. It is time we who are called leaders, to become true 'fathers of the faith,' focused upon our role of raising 'sons' of the faith, who are fully able to extend the Kingdom of God wherever they go in life.

Chapter 8

Establish
Create The Culture

Establish
Create The Culture

In war, when an army invades another nation, the first thing it endeavours to do is establish a base-camp to act as a launchpad for further deeper invasion. Their next step is to set up their defences around the base-camp to enable them to have a foothold into that country. Once the foothold is established, they move step by step into the nation. The key is to establish and secure a base, a strong-hold, to operate from. This is God's pattern on establishing His kingdom in the life of every new believer. He begins with a seed, the Word of God, which must take root and become established in order to produce the fruit of His kingdom;

Mark 4:20
"But these are the ones sown on good ground, those who hear the word, accept it, and bear fruit: some thirtyfold, some sixty, and some a hundred."

2 Timothy 1:13-14
"Hold fast the pattern of sound words which you have heard from me, in faith and love which are in Christ Jesus. That good thing which was committed to you, keep by the Holy Spirit who dwells in us."

It is also the Devil's pattern for deception;

Genesis 3:4-5
"Then the serpent said to the woman, "You will not surely die. For God knows that in the day you eat of it your eyes will be opened, and you will be like God, knowing good and evil."

The serpent actually did nothing to cause Adam and Eve to sin. All he did was say words that created doubt in their hearts and the doubt opened the door to temptation. Adam and Eve yielded to the temptation and their innocence was replaced with the guilt of their disobedience. Sin therefore took hold of man and became a stronghold that took the very blood, death and resurrection of Jesus to break. But it began with Adam and Eve receiving words.

It must become our pattern to invade society with the message and culture of the Kingdom;

> *Luke 10:1-7*
> *"After these things the Lord appointed seventy others also, and sent them two by two before His face into every city and place where He Himself was about to go. Then He said to them, The harvest truly is great, but the labourers are few; therefore pray the Lord of the harvest to send out labourers into His harvest. Go your way; behold, I send you out as lambs among wolves. Carry neither money bag, knapsack, nor sandals; and greet no one along the road. But whatever house you enter, first say, 'Peace to this house.' And if a son of peace is there, your peace will rest on it; if not, it will return to you. And remain in the same house, eating and drinking such things as they give, for the labourer is worthy of his wages. Do not go from house to house. Whatever city you enter, and they receive you, eat such things as are set before you. And heal the sick there, and say to them, The kingdom of God has come near to you.' "*

Act As a Kingdom Community

Once we have nurtured a believer into being **equipped** for the Mission, then we must help them **establish** their God-given Mission, so that it is firmly founded on Christ and can withstand the wiles of the Devil (Ephesians 6:11). The role of the Kingdom community is to surround and support them, to ensure the Mission is successfully planted and becomes a stronghold for Jesus in a segment of society. This equipped believer is now like a special forces soldier invading the enemy's territory. Therefore, they must not go alone. When they invade, then the whole of the Kingdom community goes with them in keeping a prayerful cover over them, giving financial support, or releasing people to go with them, in order to help them fulfil their Mission. We do not leave them isolated to do it alone. When one goes, we all go, acting just like a physical body.

When your hand reaches out to pick something up, then your whole body adjusts, moves, rebalances and sends brain signals, in order for the hand to do it. Your muscles torque, your sinews react, your lungs inhale more fervently, so that more oxygen is pumped into your heart, to release the energy needed to accomplish the task. It may be the hand that physically grasped the object, but everything within the body actually took part in the effort. So it must be for us in the Kingdom.

In my book *"Alignment For Assignment - Doorkeepers of God's Treasury,"* I try to clearly convey, that the early Church did not fulfil the Great Commission by building big Church buildings and establishing a system of meetings within its four walls. Instead, the early Church grew big Christians. Big Church is the result of BIG Christians. A faithful Church is the fruit of faith-full Christians. Great leadership instil's God's greatness into His people. It is time we put our total focus on people, not buildings and institutions. The early Church did not have Church buildings as we know them. They operated predominantly from homes. A persons home became the discipleship centre, which multiplied itself until discipleship cells operated all over the city or region. The home became the 'base-camp' they launched out from.

They did not operate as independent individuals, but as a collective family unit. This is the real meaning of the word 'Ecclesia,' which is the Greek word for 'Church.' A group of people in a city collectively operating as one unit, with one purpose - to establish and restore the culture of God's Kingdom in every home, street and city.

The Discipleship Cell Culture

When a sperm cell enters the woman's womb, it does so with great speed. It uses all its strength to get to its destiny and connect with the woman's egg to fertilise it. Once it has made a definite connection, it instantly multiplies itself rapidly (*There are videos on the internet that depict the incredible speed this happens*).

Daily this new life multiplies and grows. The one cell becomes many cells, creating a 'culture' of itself within the womb. The woman's immune system instantly goes into action to repel what it thinks is a foreign body or infection (morning sickness). But if this new culture, within the womb is strong enough, then it withstands the immune system's reactions and continues to not just grow, but also greatly effect the woman's body and life (tiredness, feeling faint, hunger, swelling in the lower abdomen). The more this 'invader' continues its multiplication, the more it effects the woman's body and life. All this is happening in the 'unseen' realm. You cannot see the cells multiplying, but you can see they are effecting everything around them as the body of the expectant mother changes shape. The cells operate together from the very beginning to form a living being.

This is how discipleship cells operated in the early Church days. They simply grew and multiplied, influencing the culture of society, by establishing the culture of the Kingdom of God everywhere they lived and worked. They multiplied within the established system of daily life, wherever they found themselves. They saw their daily life as an opportunity to share and demonstrate this heavenly message and culture in their neighbourhood and workplace. They influenced societies so much, that the political, business, religious and governmental bodies felt threatened that they would lose their power and control in that region. So persecution arose to prevent the growth of this new culture called 'the Kingdom of God.' These bodies tried to evict this new 'body' called 'The Kingdom of God" from taking root within their communities. But persecution had the opposite effect. It made the church even more fervent and stronger, influencing people even greater;

> *Acts 8:4-8*
> *"Therefore those who were scattered went everywhere preaching the word. Then Philip went down to the city of Samaria and preached Christ to them. And the multitudes with one accord heeded the things spoken by Philip, hearing and seeing the miracles which he did. For unclean spirits, crying with a loud voice, came out of many who were possessed; and many who were paralysed and lame were healed. And there was great joy in that city."*

> *Acts 11:19-21*
> *"Now those who were scattered after the persecution that arose over Stephen traveled as far as Phoenicia, Cyprus, and Antioch, preaching the word to no one but the Jews only. But some of them*

*were men from Cyprus and Cyrene, who, when they had come to
Antioch, spoke to the Hellenists, preaching the Lord Jesus. And the
hand of the Lord was with them, and a great number believed and
turned to the Lord."*

(See also Acts 4:18-33).

The persecution led to the growth of the Church. Why? Because the unsaved
people of the region watched the response of Christians to persecution, the
knowledge of their certain death or torture, and also to their persecutors.
They saw the love the Church had for Jesus and one another, visibly
demonstrated before them. They watched as Christians forgave those who
tortured, butchered and robbed them of their earthly possessions. They
saw Christians thrown into arenas and be attacked by lions, whilst at the
same time lifting their hands and voices, audibly praising Jesus Christ, and
thanking Him for His great forgiveness and mercy, whilst also praying for
God's mercy towards their persecutors. The unsaved population watched the
culture of Heaven operating on earth, amongst those known as 'the Church,'
who freely gave up everything they had and forgave everyone who rejected
and persecuted them, because they loved Christ, not their earthly lives, even
to the end (Rev 12:11).

Heaven On Earth - The Will Of The Father
Jesus didn't die so we could all go to Heaven. He died so Heaven could be
restored to earth. Adam walked with God on earth (Genesis 3:8). Father did
not create Adam and take him to Heaven. He fashioned Heaven on Earth
and placed Adam into it. Before they sinned, Adam and Eve experienced
the perfect culture of Heaven, on earth. It was their sin that caused Father
to put them outside that environment and close the door that locked all of
mankind out of the Garden. He did so fully knowing His Son would come
to earth, die on the cross to pay the cost of all sin through His own death, for
this door to be reopened, to all who accept Christ as their Saviour.

As Jesus breathed His last breath on the cross, so the veil that hung in the
Temple separating the Most Holy Place from the Holy Place, was torn from
top to bottom declaring the way into Fathers presence and Heavens culture,
had been reopened, through His grace and mercy.

If you were suddenly transported into Heaven right now, what do you think it would be like? Would you see hatred, revenge, bitterness, division, ego, skin colour or denominations? You know you wouldn't, because Jesus is not like that, nor is His Kingdom. The Kingdom of Heaven is an exact copy of the King of Heaven.

Jesus taught His disciples to pray:

> *"Your kingdom come, Your will be done on earth as it is in Heaven."*
> *(Matt 6:10)*

Before we can establish God's Kingdom on Earth as it is in Heaven, then we must first be thoroughly sure we know what it is like, and is not like, in Heaven.

You cannot have the Kingdom of God apart from having His will. They go together and are inseparable. Heaven is the complete manifestation of the will of God. In Heaven there is no sin, sickness, disease, demons, fear, brokenness, rejection, black, white, rich or poor. There is no understanding of denominations, ego, pride, or division. All are totally committed to being the living expression of God's unconditional love as a community of worshippers of Jesus. This is Heavens culture. Therefore, the will of God is to establish and manifest this same culture on earth, within the community of those called according to His purposes - the Church.

Father desires to see healings and miracles happening in His Church. But He wants us to believe for something even greater. He wants us to believe for total wholeness for all people inside and outside of the Church. He wants the Church to be free of the demonic control of fear. But He desires we go further than this and operate like Jesus and destroy the works of darkness. He wants us to go into the world of fear and bring deliverance to all controlled and bound by it. He wants us to continue to operate like His special forces, sent out of Heaven to invade every section of society in the earth, evicting the evil dictator and his forces, which is the Devil, Demons and Deception, and in their place, establish His Kingdom culture.

Dear friend, hear me clearly today. Establishing discipleship cells across the city or region, with the clear goal to manifest His Kingdom culture amongst and through a Kingdom minded family unit, is the organic, God-given method, that enables us to fill the earth with the culture of Heaven. It is how the Kingdom of God grows and flourishes in the earth (Genesis 1:22, 28; Genesis 9:1; Genesis 22:17; Exodus 1:9-19; Isaiah 9:6-8)

Habakkuk 2:14
"For the earth will be filled with the knowledge of the glory of the Lord, as the waters cover the sea."

Whatever someone's 'Mission' is, it must have this same goal in mind.

Chapter 9

Energise
Release The Resources

Energise
Release The Resources

To equip someone to do their Mission and teach them to operate in the delegated authority of Jesus, but not help them with the resources to start their Mission, is planing to fail. We must supply people with the resources to do their Mission wherever necessary.

Maybe what I am about to say is going to shock you. To resource people to achieve their God-given Mission, is the real purpose of tithes. Tithes are not meant to be used for building projects, with glitzy auditoriums and their utility bills. The tithes are for providing 'food' in the House of God;

> *Malachi 3:8-10*
> *"Bring all the tithes into the storehouse, that there may be food in My house,"*

The tithes paid in the Old Testament were most often results of the harvest of flocks or crops. The tithe of the harvest was taken to the temple and given to the priests. It was to provide food for those working in the Temple.

In 2 Kings 22:3-9, King Josiah gives instruction regarding the money stored in the Temple Treasury;

> *"deliver it into the hand of those **doing the work** who are **the overseers** in the House of the Lord, let them give it to the those in the House of the Lord, **who are doing the work, to repair the damages of the House.**"*

Notice, the tithes were given to those who oversee the work, and the overseers gave it to the ones actually doing the work in the House of the

Lord (the Temple). The key seen here, is the resources to do the job were given to the ones who actually did the work. What is the 'work' of the New Testament Temple? Is it not to make Jesus known in all the earth, and the discipling of all nations?

In the Old Testament the Temple is a physical building. In the New Testament the Temple of God is a spiritual Temple made up of all who are born again;

> *1 Corinthians 3:16-17*
> *"Do you not know that you are the temple of God and that the Spirit of God dwells in you? If anyone defiles the temple of God, God will destroy him. For the temple of God is holy, which temple you are."*

The Old Testament priest came from the tribe of Levi. In the New Testament all born again believers are called the 'royal priesthood'

> *1 Pet 2:5, 9*
> *"you also, as living stones, are being built up a spiritual house, a holy priesthood, to offer up spiritual sacrifices acceptable to God through Jesus Christ........v9 But you are a chosen generation, a royal priesthood, a holy nation,"*

When someone is fruitful in the mission of reaching the unsaved with the gospel bringing new believers into the Kingdom of God, then these new believers are being added by the Holy Spirit into the Temple of God. So the eternal Temple is extended, and continues to grow and be added to. This is New Testament ministry. Therefore, if the tithes are meant to be used to build, restore the House of God and resource the priesthood, then the New Testament tithes, or offerings, can be given to help Christians, who through their God-given Mission, reach people with the Gospel of Jesus and disciple them.

Once again I think I may shock you with this next statement. The finances of the early Church were always given into the hands of **apostles.** It does not say 'pastors'

> *"Nor was there anyone among them who lacked; for all who were possessors of lands, or houses, sold them, and brought the proceeds*

*of the things that were sold, and laid them at the **apostles** feet, and they distributed to each as anyone had need." (Acts 4:34-37;*

You may feel I am simply 'splitting hairs' in saying the finances of the day were given to the apostles, not the pastors. I promise you I am not desperate to find a way to simply challenge a traditional viewpoint. The biblical expression of pastoral ministry is explained in it's very name.

The Meaning of 'Pastor.'

Ephesians 4:11
"And He Himself gave some to be apostles, some prophets, some evangelists, and some pastors and teachers,"

The word 'pastor,' used by Paul is '*poimen*,' which means 'shepherd.' The word shepherd comes from combining the two words 'sheep' and 'herder.' He, or she, is the herder of the sheep. They are the ones focussed on the feeding, health and protection of the flock, whilst leading them from pasture to pasture.

The Meaning of Apostle
The word 'apostle,' used by Paul in the same verse, is *apostello*, meaning 'set apart, sent out, an ambassador.' Its original use was for the title of the Captain of a ship that was sent overseas to establish a new colony. On board his ship were the people and cargo in order to achieve the mission the apostle had been sent to achieve. The word *'apostello'* actually carries the meaning that not just the Captain was sent, but also the ship, the cargo and the people were all 'sent' to do this work. The apostles were sent with one purpose. They were to establish a colony on behalf of the one who sent them, and the colony was to be established in such a way that it exactly reflected the culture of the one who sent them to go and establish the new colony.

The Difference Between The Two Ministries
Pastors are concerned with the welfare of the ones already within the sheep-fold. Apostles are also concerned with the sheep already within the fold, because the apostles are the ones who plant the new 'colonies' (the church cell). But they are also just as concerned with multiplying the colonies of God's Kingdom, and extending the Kingdom of God wherever it is not yet

established. The apostles want to duplicate what they have already planted.

These ministries are not in contention. They operate together as a team, so that the new colony is planted and taken care of, whilst at the same time it is duplicated elsewhere. One cares for what is already established, so that those called to go further and establish new colonies can do so, safely knowing the pastoral team are looking after the 'colony' the apostles have already established.

The pastoral ministry is concerned with the 'local' church, while the apostolic ministry is concerned with the 'regional' church. The local and regional church are one and the same church. They are not different churches. The pastors care that the one cell operates properly, whilst the apostles care for the multiple cells co-operating together properly. Each planted cell resources the apostles, and the other ministries, to expand and develop the work of God in the region and in other nations.

This is the reason, I believe, the tithes and offerings were laid at the apostles feet. They carry the responsibility to establish the bigger picture, the fuller expression of the Kingdom of God. Therefore, they release the finances to achieve the whole work, not just the local work. Maybe the work of establishing the culture of Heaven in every aspect of society, would happen easier and quicker if we did this same thing today.

Could today's church system cope operating on just 10% of their income from tithes, releasing 90% to extend the Kingdom of God through the work of apostles? I doubt it to be possible in most places, doing church the way it is normally done. But it could be easily done if we adopted the New Testament model of church, established through discipleship cells. Then, most of the tithes and offerings could be given into the hands of apostles to be used for its intended purpose, to build and restore God's living Temple across the city, region and nation.

Chapter 10

Ensure
Oversight Is Not Control

Ensure
Oversight Is Not Control

It is the purpose for all in a place of ministry leadership, to ensure to provide on-going spiritual oversight and support, to all who step out to fulfil their mission.

The more you have genuinely Equipped, Engaged and Energised individuals to achieve their Mission from the beginning, the less you will need to do to help them in the long-term. But you will need to continue to give on-going loving support to them, because everyone who steps out to fulfil their Mission has to resist and endure the spiritual battle that contends with them in order to prevent the Mission being established.

To give oversight means, to 'see-over,' or 'watch-over' in a protective way. It does not mean dictate, command or keep control over people. In my book *'Alignment For Assignment,'* I show clearly that the model of leadership mostly operating in todays Church life, is not the kind of Church leadership model revealed in the New Testament. Most Church leadership models operating today are based on a hierarchal structured, pastor lead model, which is not the New Testament model of leadership.

New Testament Team Ministry
In the hierarchal model there is one man, or woman, in control, who has the title 'pastor,' who usually gives out the vision for everyone else to build. Under them are a group of 2nd Tier leaders, often called 'Elders,' followed by a 3rd Tier of leaders often called 'Deacons.' The system is basically a pyramid style of ministry and authority. Those at the top do more and have more authority than those underneath. This is absolutely not the model laid down by Jesus and revealed in the Book of Acts or the Letters to the Churches. (*Please see my book 'Alignment For Assignment' for a more in-depth look at this subject*)

Leadership in the New Testament Church model, is always seen operating in the plural, or team sense. No leader operated in isolation, or was in 'charge' on their own. They followed the model of Jesus in working in two's, or in a team. Accountability is absolutely essential for every leader. Accountability balances and protects the individual leader and the flock from the destructive excesses that often are the result of misunderstanding of what genuine authority is and how it must be operated in the work of the Kingdom of God.

Also, the New Testament leaders never used the five-fold ministry as positions or titles. They knew them to be descriptive of a persons ministry purpose and function only. All five-fold ministry recognised themselves as part of a team of Elders who gave 'oversight' to the work of God in a region, not inside a Church building (Titus 1:5; 1Pet 5:1; 2 John 1:1).

God gives leaders grace and authority for a purpose. It is to lift others up to full potential, not to raise up their own ministry by making others subservient to themselves. Jesus came down from Heaven, laying aside all of His glory and divinity to become as man, to lay down His life as our ransom, in order to deliver us all from the burden and slavery to sin and death. All who received Him as their Lord and Saviour were placed in Jesus Christ at the right-hand of the Father. His style of leadership is to get underneath people to raise them up to His stature, not vice versa.

New Testament leaders didn't have a preplanned, organised set of activities of what they believed God would do, and therefore operate and co-ordinate it all. They understood it was the Holy Spirit that was actually the One building the Church, daily adding people to it (Acts 2:47), and leading people to places to extend the Kingdom (Acts 8:26-40). They simply responded to what He was doing, wherever He was doing it, and at the time He chose to do it. I have said for many years, we would be much more fruitful if we simply learnt to work where He is working, when He is working, with whom He is working, not trying to persuade Him to work where and when we want Him to.

Organic Leadership Pattern
The task of leaders is to prepare a people who can continue to extend the work, of establishing the Kingdom of God in the hearts of people

everywhere. Then, to release them to the care of the Holy Spirit in order to do it, praying for them and giving any other support necessary, in order to help them achieve their Mission;

> *Acts 13:2-4*
> *"As they ministered to the Lord and fasted, the Holy Spirit said, "Now separate to Me Barnabas and Saul for the work to which I have called them." Then, having fasted and prayed, and laid hands on them, they sent them away."*

> *Ch 14:23*
> *"So when they had appointed elders in every church, and prayed with fasting, they commended them to the Lord in whom they had believed."*

This, once again, is revealed in the organic natural way of doing life. We raise children to get married, with the ability to raise a family of their own, in their own home, under their own authority and responsibility. Once they leave the parents home, the role of the parent changes to one of support, lovingly watching out to give them any help they should need, and quietly and humbly pointing out any danger signs you can see along the way. At no time do we 'take over,' or demand they do something that we think they should do.

Everything we do must flow out of loving support and wisdom, not power based titles or authority. My friend, if you have genuine authority, then people will recognise it and receive it. If you have to shout, intimidate or manipulate people, using your title or position to make them do what you want, then you really don't have any authority in their lives at all. People may respond and do what you say, but it will be out of a fear of you, not out of recognising the wisdom of God you carry.

Jesus promised to send to us 'The Comforter,' who is the Holy Spirit. The word 'comforter' is the Greek word *'parakletos,'* which means to come alongside, to help give you support and consolation, in times of need. This is such a beautiful example of heavenly leadership, that we all would do well to imitate. Let us have this same Spirit that was in Christ Jesus, and come alongside people to give support when they need it, not treat people as if they are less than us and under our authority.

Always remember, people are not our children and they are not our sheep, but His. He is their Father and Shepherd and we are their siblings in Christ and His under-shepherds. He desires to speak to their hearts directly and personally shepherd them along life's journey. If we can bring every believer to the place to know Father intimately for themselves, and be able to recognise His voice, feed themselves from His Word, walk with Him and make Him known to people, then we have done a great job.

A wise friend of mine gave me a great piece of wisdom in my early days of ministry, that remained with me all these years. He reminded me that a shepherd in biblical times, built a sheep-pen with an entrance, and then personally slept in that entrance to protect the sheep from wolves or bears. But the shepherd never built a roof over the top of the pen. The sheep could always look up to the heavens whenever they wanted to. The flock of God must always be able to look to, and talk to Him for themselves, not through any earthly mediator, for He is their Chief Shepherd and cares for them and knows the way they should go, more than any other person (Thank you Mel Morgan).

Finally, as I said earlier in the book, let us dare to be brave enough to change from operating an unfruitful organisation and begin to unleash a self-multiplying, self-propelling organism, that can reach this worlds population in just 40 years. It could take just 40 years to reach over 7 Billion people if we dare do it His way. But we will never achieve the goal doing Church the way we do it now. It is time to change. This change is called 'Reformation,' and it has already begun. So join it, not fight it, for you will be fighting against Jesus and the work of His Kingdom.

Chapter 11

Enrol
Others Can Help

Enrol
Others Can Help

What Now? I hear some of you saying after reading this book. Many times I have listened to leaders tell me that they have known for years that this new move of God was coming, but never realised it would be a reformation in the way Church operated. Many agree the Church must radically change from a structure of organisation to organism. It is not this that concerns leaders everywhere. What concerns so many is the 'how do we do it?' Maybe that is how you feel right now. Then why not simply join us at *in*HOPE and get connected to people around the world all going in the same direction.

Here at *in*HOPE we have been preparing for this new reformation, and still are doing so, and therefore have many insights that will help you bring the relevant changes and adjustments necessary. But let me leave you with one word of wisdom. The larger the ministry or Church work, the harder and slower the change will be. In some places, to bring this radical change may be impossible. Therefore you may need to consider a brand new independent work, or a new work that runs alongside the old one until the old fades away.

If you are out in your canoe or dingy boat, then to turn and change direction is easy. But if you are the Captain of a large ocean-going vessel, then decisions can be made easily to change course, but the time it takes to accomplish this change of course is obviously much longer. It depends upon the size of the vessel, or in our case, the Church or ministry.

The longer the Church work, or ministry has been established, then the deeper the roots of tradition are and the harder it will be to uproot the old practices, concepts and mind-set of Church or ministry from the people. You must renew the peoples mindset;

Ephesians 4:22-24
"that you put off, concerning your former conduct, the old man
*which grows corrupt according to the deceitful lusts, and be **renewed***
***in the spirit of your mind**, and that you put on the new man which*
was created according to God, in true righteousness and holiness."

Proverbs 23:7
*"For as he **thinks** in his heart, so is he."*

Mindsets are heart issues and out of the heart flow the issues, or forces of life;

Proverbs 4:23
"Keep your heart with all diligence,
For out of it spring the issues of life."

Our 'heart' is the seat of our will and to bring change means I need my will, deep rooted desires and beliefs to change. This can only happen when I am convinced I have heard the truth. So we need to give people plenty of time to hear, read and be convicted that this change called 'reformation' is truly of the Lord. Then we can all activate our faith in this 'new word' from the Spirit and move forward into all it means. Some are ready for it right now. Others around you may need a bit more time to adjust. They are not against you - they just need more time than others to digest this new concept of Church life. There are also those that almost refuse to change. The key is to love them all to the same measure and pray constantly over all the people involved, trying always to reassure people that they can trust Jesus implicitly in such a way that trust can be developed, enabling them to move forward and actually enjoy the life-changing and enjoyable rewards of walking with Jesus into this new season.

We are in this together. You are not alone, even if at times, like Elijah (1 Kings 19:10-18), you feel like you are. You are not. There are others in this with you.

Revival Or Reformation?
I am from Wales, a nation known around the world as the Land of Revival. It is because we have had more revivals than any other nation and the

major revival of 1904 swept right through Wales impacting every aspect of society, bringing radical changes everywhere. This revival spread right around the world and was a major influence on those used of God to birth the pentecostal movement in Los Angeles.

So when I am ministering in the nations I am always asked to share what I know about the 1904 revival. Of course I willingly respond to such requests, sharing incredible examples of how the revival impacted society so much. But I always finish by saying that I personally am not praying or wanting another revival in Wales. This of course shocks everyone, because it seems the Church everywhere, is desperate to have one, believing it to be the answer to everything. It is not! To revive something, or someone, is simply to bring back to life something that has died. In a sense to simply wake it back up.

When believers pray for a revival, what they are looking for is for the Church to experience the move of God like it did in former days. But you can walk or drive around Wales today and see no evidence of all that happened in the greatest revival of 1904. In fact, there is a statue of Evan Roberts the revivalist that was the main figure in the 1904 revival, right outside the Church building mostly known as the hub of the revival. Yet unsaved people walk past his statue and have no idea who Evan Roberts was, or that this great revival happened in their small town!

I do not pray the Lord raise back up the Church to operate as it did in those days. That revival died within a few short years through lack of prepared leadership and revolved around meetings instead of discipleship. The revival simply died away and normal Church life and activity reverted back to as it was before. No, I don't want this to happen again in my nation or any other nation. There must come a reformation. Look at this word again. A re-form-ation;

> Mark 16:12-13
> "After that, He appeared in **another form** to two of them as they walked and went into the country. And they went and told it to the rest, but they did not believe them either."

I explain in my book "Alignment For Assignment" that one day, after being a believer and in full-time ministry for many years, my eyes were opened on re-reading these two verses in Marks Gospel. *"Another form"* leapt off the page, as if I was reading it for the very first time. The truth is that I had read this passage a multitude of times, but I **was** reading it as if for the first time. It was the first time my eyes were opened and my thinking was challenged to the meaning of those two words, *'another form.'*

I remember getting out my Strong's Concordance reference book, my Young's literal translation study book and other such research books. I needed to understand what could Mark really mean when writing this statement. Surely Jesus didn't change His appearance. Did He? Could He?

When writing this statement Mark uses the Greek word *'morphe.'* Strong's Concordance reveals this word 'morphe' means, 'the adjustment of shape, form or nature.' The word 'form' is the root for the word 'format.'

In the 1960's and 70's I, like all of my friends, listened to music on vinyl records. But suddenly there was a new and easier way to listen to your favourite singers or bands. It was called the cassette tape. To play the cassette tape you had to have a special new cassette player. You could not use the vinyl record in a cassette player, nor the cassette tape on a record player. Why? Because they were of different formats. The same thing happened when CD's were launched and today we need no such items as vinyl records, cassettes or CD's, because we can listen to all our music via a phone, a computer or a 'virtual assistant' in our homes that streams all music directly from the internet. The formats keep changing and when it does, then the old format is obsolete and will not work with the new one.

If the Father had simply revived Jesus, then He would have come back to life, looking and being exactly as He was when they buried Him three days before. But Father didn't revive Jesus. Mark tells us the Jesus who came out of the tomb had completely changed form. What went into the grave is not what came out! The old was gone forever and the new had come.

The Resurrection Was A Reformation

Jesus was so different that repeatedly the apostles and those closest to Him, did not even recognise Him by appearance. He did things after His death that He never did before. He disappeared and re-appeared elsewhere and kept changing His appearance. He walked in and out of walls, seemingly at leisure.

His Church is His Body on earth. We are born again not after the nature of the One who they placed into the tomb, but after the nature of the One who rose from the dead. The resurrection was not a revival, but a full blown reformation and this new reformation demanded the apostles and disciples to change their understanding on the way Jesus wanted everything done.

I am totally convinced by the Spirit, that Father is moving today right across the Church in the nations, looking for and preparing individuals to work together to bring another reformation. A reformation in the way we do Church entirely. As I have already said, reformation is not for the faint-hearted, but for those with a courage and conviction to bring the changes so necessary to Church structure, concept and life, in order to fulfil His greatest desire to see all men saved everywhere, and the restoration of all things on earth, back into alignment with His glorious Kingdom.

The question is: do you want to be a revivalist or a reformer?

Further Information

Books:
Don't Kick The Donkey-Ride it!   ISBN 978-0-9567277-0-1
Alignment For Assignment   ISBN 978-0-9567277-0-8

Web Site: www.wynnegoss.com
Our website contains in-depth information about the lives and ministry of Wynne & Gwenda, their ministry schedule, free samples of their songs and tv recordings.

Connect:
Each week Wynne and Gwenda send out an email giving links to their internet TV programs, which are all free. Their passion is to give away over 40 years of ministry insight, teaching materials and wisdom, to Christians in every nation. To receive them, please go to our website www.wynnegoss.com and sign up.

You can also connect with Wynne via Facebook and Twitter.

Donations:
Wynne & Gwenda's ministry is entirely supported from the generosity of those around the world who have been touched by God's grace, through their ministry. If you would like to help their mission, you can use the PayPal button on their website.

Contact:
You can contact Wynne or Gwenda by emailing them at info@wynnegoss.com

Other Titles by Wynne Goss

Don't Kick the Donkey ... Ride It!

'Don't Kick The Donkey ... Ride it!', Wynne's first book, reveals how the hand of God is forever involved in the processes that turn negative situations into ones that conform you to His likeness, allowing you to see everything through His perspective, enabling you to overcome the obstacles and mountains of adversity, to achieve His destiny for your life. You will clearly find 'letting go of everything you have ever known, to lay hold of everything you have ever dreamed of,' is not just a chapter title, but a way of life being offered to the reader.

Alignment for Assignment - Door Keepers of God's Treasury

"Let Your Kingdom come in earth, as it is in Heaven" was never meant to be a repetitive prayer, but rather a constant awareness that this is the Father's perfect plan for every moment of your life. Heaven is constantly pressing to invade the world through you with it's power, to re-align all things back into the order of His perfect Kingdom.

'Alignment For Assignment' is an apostolic message calling the Church to embrace true reformation and realignment to the New Testament model of Christianity, to achieve an uncontainable and unlimited flow of the Spirit resulting in global evangelism and discipleship of all nations.